Vendors Jubilee Magazine

Copyright © 2018 Life Empowerment Publishing

All rights reserved.

ISBN-13: **978-1985790667**

ISBN-10: **1985790661**

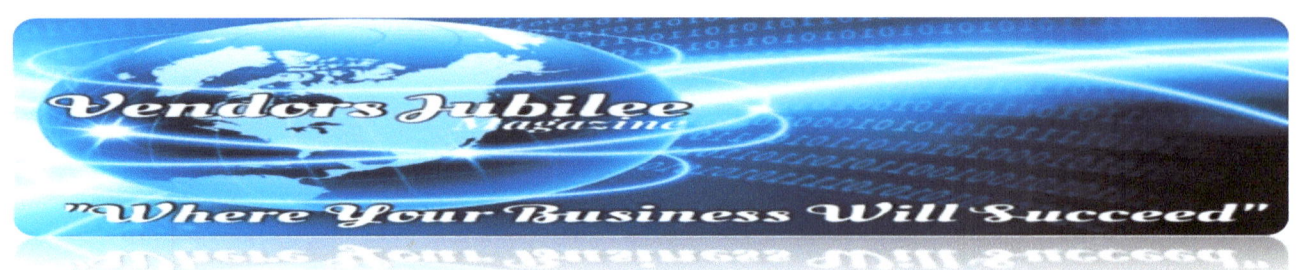

Just -Understanding-Business-In-Life-Everyday-Events

Mission/Vision:

To help aid in accomplishing entrepreneur's growth within their business establishment. To help consumers to purchase, join and applying Kingdom building to edify growth within our communities, cities, and states.

Shamika Curry founder CEO, Vendors Jubilee, along with her husband Joseph M. Curry

Vendors Jubilee was founded in 2016 location Jacksonville Florida and now resides in Fairview Heights Illinois. Our Global establishment is design with entrepreneurs like yourself in mind, to help aid and establish growth within your business. It's our company delight to assist your business to success with a high-volume flow of customers to your business establishment. It's our business to make sure your business succeeds.

We believe, at Vendors Jubilee your business will Succeed!

VENDORS JUBILEE

Dear Valued Customer

Vendors Jubilee Magazine is delighted, you decided to market your business "Better Wear Custom Apparel."

Our magazine was created to help aid in entrepreneurs' growth within their business establishment. Every, business owner, vendors, communities, church, and conference events are structure to establish consumers to purchase, join, and apply Kingdom building to edify growth within our communities, cities and states. This magazine issue will be distributed quarterly.

This is a global magazine, will be available on amazon, other online merchant stores, local boutiques, doctors' offices, beauty salons in Metro East and St Louis Mo area. Just to name a couple other states Georgia, Florida, Texas, and many more.

Vendors Jubilee magazine first issue will be released on March 2018 through June 2018

Your ad will be available throughout the years. Please send your ad information to: vendorsjubileemagazine@gmail.com

www.vendorsjubilee.com

Thank you for your support, we can impact the world with economic growth within our communities for God's Glory!

We honor and appreciate our customers!

Thank you,

Mrs. Shamika Curry
Founder CEO
Pastor Joseph Curry
 Editor- In- Chief
Vendors Jubilee Magazine

MYSTIQUEE AGENCY

MANY

YOUNG

STYLE

TALENT

INCORPORATED

QUALITY

UNIQUENESS

EVOLV-ING

EVERYDAY

Agency

Model Shamika Wilkins

Please Send Picture to:

mystiqueeagencyevents@gmail.com

$50.00 Registration Fee Payment:

www.paypal.me/MystiqueeAgency

You will be contacted for an interview!

"Model the Light of The World"

Modeling AGENCY

Mystiquee Agency

Professional Talent Model Agency.

We offer:

Catalog
Commercials
Fashion Show

Wedding Events Coordinator Services

(904) 661 – 9253

Terianna Brooks
"God's Songbird"

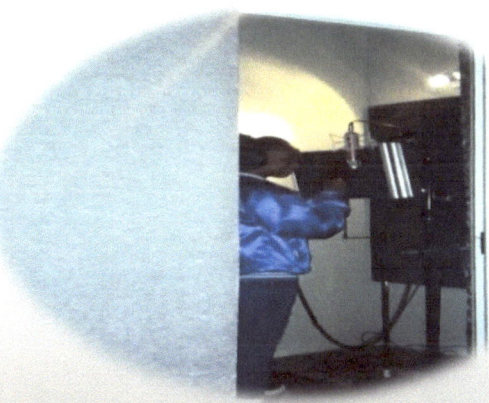

"Truth Be Told" Cd Coming Soon, with her debut single "Truth is The Light"

For more Information, Please Contact necipoohzboutique@gmail.com
Coming soon 2018

Contents

WANT TO BE A MODEL?

Mystiquee Agency   [4]
Looking For You!

Where You Are the Star!

Better Wear Custom Apparel
We Give You Best Quality Printing!
Owner: Jhonny Salano   [17]

Dr. Emita Williams   [11]

"Power of Focus"

Dr. Nikki Weiss   *{22}*
Healthy + Happy
Choose healthy living and discover a new you!

Sell or Buy your Home Today!

Whitney Wisnasky-Bettorf   [12]
Courtney Marsh

The Lion & Lamb Music   [16]
Father Crop
DeAndre Thompson

Pastor Joseph M. Curry
"Man with a Vision"
Film Director
"Locker Room the Movie"

Minister Cynthia Newell   [18]
R.I.S.E. & W.I.N.
"Woman on a Mission from GOD"

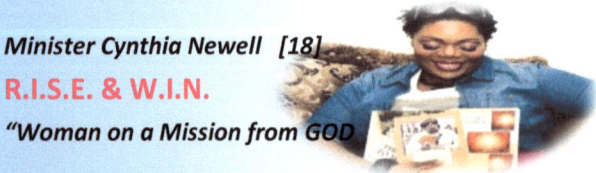

Go Check out Locker Room The Movie Cast Articles

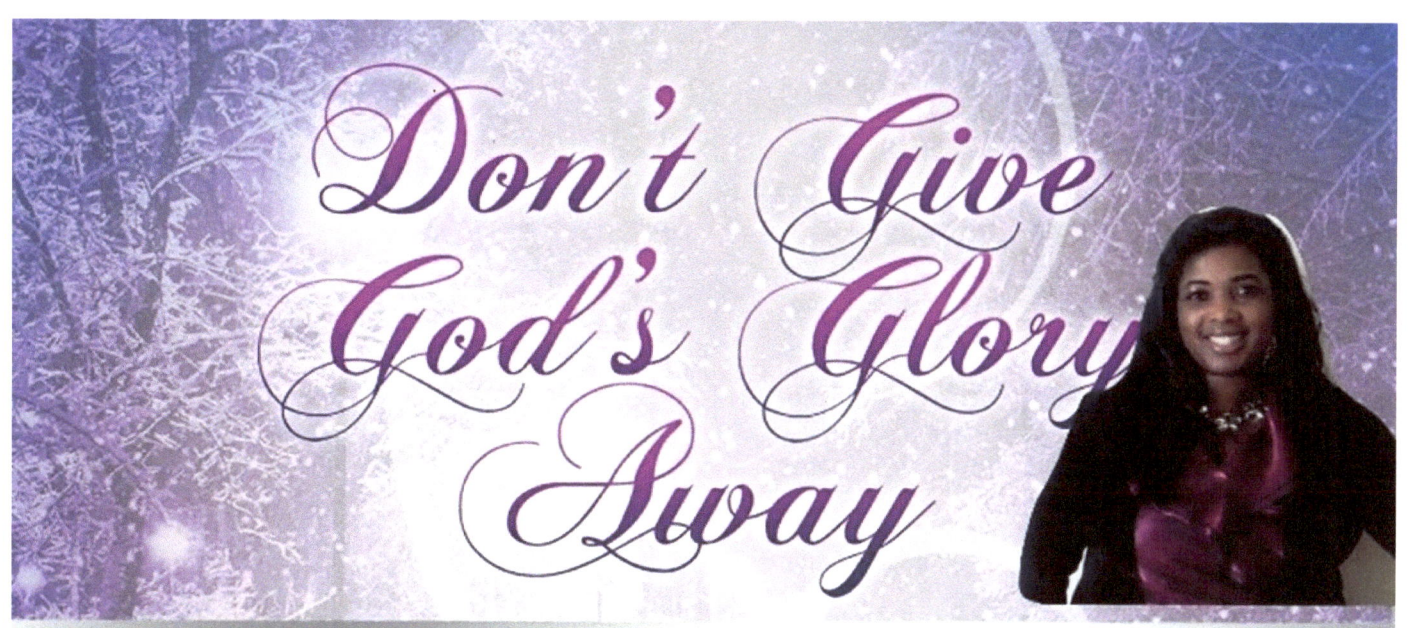

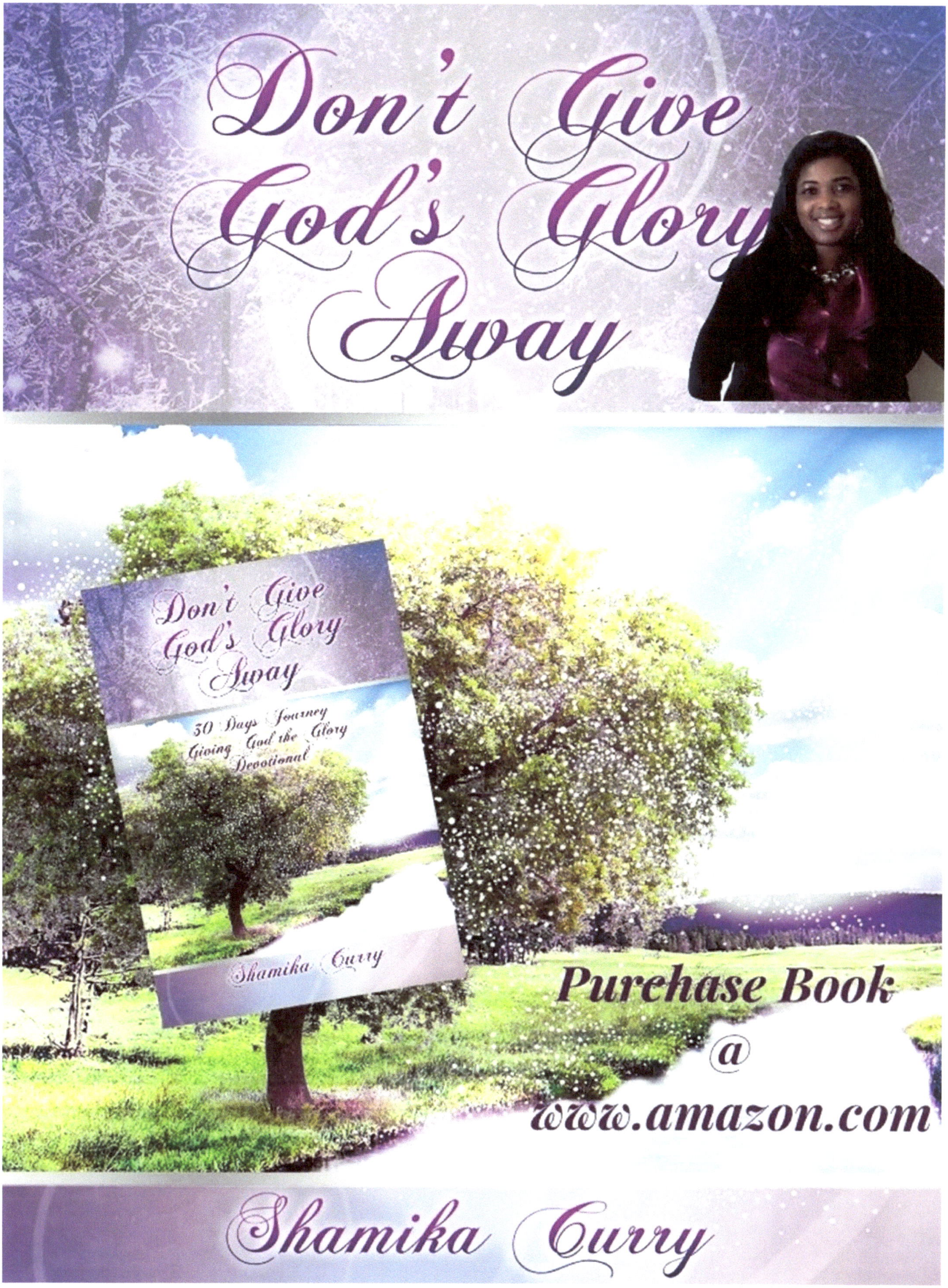
Don't Give God's Glory Away
Don't Give God's Glory Away
30 Days Journey Giving God the Glory Devotional
Shamika Curry
Purchase Book
@
www.amazon.com
Shamika Curry

For more Information or to be a Guess on the Show,
please send all inquiries to
breakingintoyourvictory@gmail.com

Dr. Emita Williams
Graduated Master's Degree Education Administration and a Doctor in Education Leadership,

Dec. 2017

She just recently Graduate December 2017 from Maryville University, and received a Master Degree Education Administration and a Doctor in Education Leadership, What inspire her to be a teacher her mother…but she did not want me to be a teacher, she wanted her to be a journalist our a news reporter, but she decided to pursue her dream to be a teacher and attended SIUE and graduated May 1999, with her Bachelors of Science in Early Childhood and May 2009, Maryville University Masters in Early Childhood. She has been teaching for 19 years now, since graduating from SIUE thanks to one of her professors; Dr. Suzie Nall introduce her to River Garden School District. Her goal now is to become a Principle or Early Child hood education Administration and become a Superintended.

Dr. Emita Williams
"The Power of Focus"

Dr. Emita Williams is a wonderful wife to Mr. Donald Williams and a mother of 7 beautiful children. She has taken on one of her passion in being a, actress in an upcoming Feature film in "Locker Room The Movie". At the age of 42 she always believe you can begin again. I will like to encourage everyone to keep God first you are never too old to fulfill your purpose because God has a plan and he won't you to not leave this earth full of your dream and be led by God.

"God is first, and my family is my second priority"

Dr. Emita believe her friend will say she is a loyal, fun loving person and like to have fun, but most of all put God first. A person of inspiration has been Oprah Winfrey, because she has an awesome testimony that has pushed herself while having a self-driven determination that keep her focus on her career in spite of all the rejection in her life. What has inspired Dr. Emita Williams to pursue her PH D, she always had a plan to pursue greater. She also like to model and be a good role model to younger women and children to help aid in others desires to pursue their dream and goal by showing them how to go after what God has in store for you to be great leaders, to position yourself around like-minded people. You have to keep God first and stay focus on the vision God has given you.

Forever Begins Today!

Mr. & Mrs. Williams

SELL OR BUY YOUR HOUSE TODAY!

Evangelist Meishel Matkins

"I Am an Overcomer"

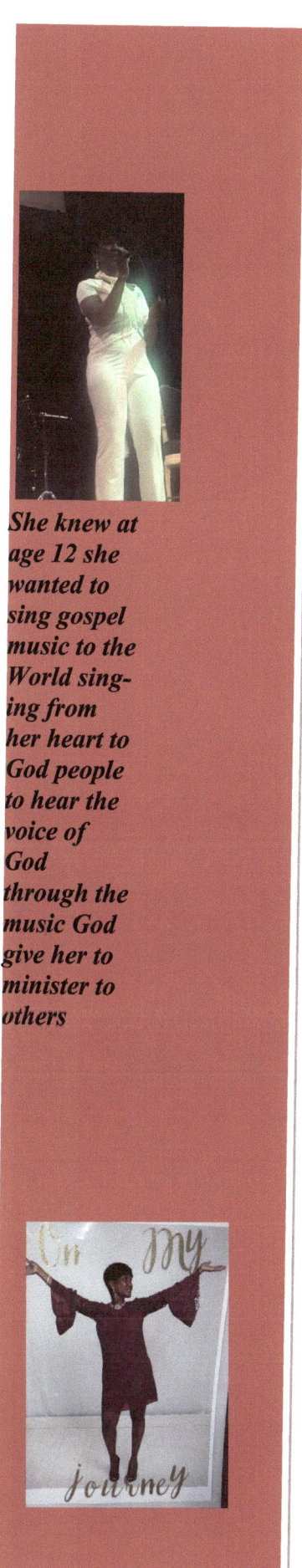

Evangelist Meishel Matkins is a native of East St Louis, Illinois, when she was 12 years old walking around singing at her grandmother's house with a broom or brush in her hands. She started singing secular music and start writing song. They did not sound right to her, so she wanted to write gospel songs instead. She said, "she can do anything through Christ that strengthen her." She is into real estate, dreams of owning her own shelter for homeless people, she had to reconnect herself to God instead of doing things her way. She asked God what her purpose was because she felt at the time she did have no direction. Feel like she was just taking a job to live pay check to pay check is not the will of God. She asked God what was her purpose and he told her to open a woman's shelter for mother and children.

Evangelist Meishel Matkins have always been a dreamer in spite her being a battered woman, she is an overcomer. Her heart and desire are to have a battered woman shelter housing for woman and their children, to be able to minister the word of God, help other woman that has been battered, even though there are battered men. The vision God has given her is to help batter women because she can relate to them. Her passion for battered woman to help them know that they are beautiful, and God will give them a safe haven and can overcome any obstacles that tries to stand in their way. Her heart desire is to help aid them to have housing and job placement to make a difference in their life. She has even more dreams to have real estate properties and a Laundromat to be able to accommodate the communities need. Open opportunities and doors to help people of God, because I believe every good dream comes from God. A couple of people she said has inspired her is Mary Mary, Prophetess Shamika Curry, her husband Pastor Joseph M. Curry, Prophetess Margret Green and so many others, if she said you have inspired her she means it.

She knew at age 12 she wanted to sing gospel music to the World singing from her heart to God people to hear the voice of God through the music God give her to minister to others

Norma Solano
"Destine for Greatness"

Ms. Norma Solano age 21, been in a movie" Locker Room The Movie" it was such an amazing experience to be working with Mr. Joseph Curry, his lovely wife Shamika and cast.

She has always wanted to be an actress this movie opportunity actual made one of her dreams come true. This is what she always wanted to be in a movie ever since she was a little girl.

Even in her young age she wants to have more opportunity to be on, T.V. shows, travel around the world.

Her project she is trying to accomplish at this moment in her life, she will like to write a book, be a singer and love to learn how to play the guitar. The book she like to write will be about helping teens to be destine for greatness. She will also like to buy her a house to help establish her family stability. She is the 7th out of 8 siblings making her second to the last youngest child.

She said her mother and father inspires her to be a better person.

They are very loyal and dedicated parent to their children and to people in general.

She is planning on traveling the world and doing more movies in the future!

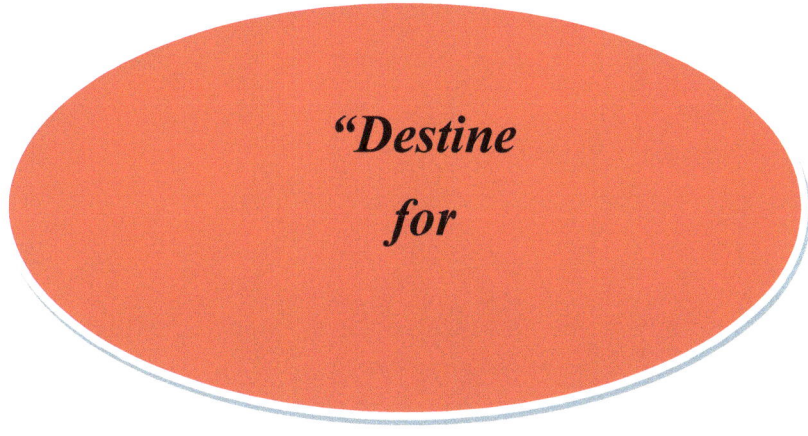

"Destine for

DREAMS DO COME TRUE

Jhonny Solano
"Design with a Purpose"

Better Wear Custom Apparel
We Give You Best Quality Printing!

1 (618) 560-2015

Facebook & Instagram
@
betterwearcustomapparel

honny Solano is 21 years old, he started his business at age 18

"Better Wear Custom Apparel." He started his business in his living room for about 3 months before he opened his own shop in September 2017 that is located 2204 State St. East St Louis IL 62201. He started making t-shirts design in 2014 working for someone else and they pushed him into opening his own shop. He did not like working for minimal wage, and for someone else, so he started his own business. He knew he had a talent that was more valuable, his passion is to customize any clothing, picture, stickers, and family reunions etc.

His dream is to be in movies, a rapper, basketball player and a business owner entrepreneur.

Business has always been in him, at the age of 15 he uses to go and shovel snow, cut grass, just to make a living. Jhonny is inspired by Bill Gates and Elon Musk. He is also the second oldest out of five children.

His five years goals is to be a millionaire, open a franchise for Better Wear Custom Apparel. He has all ways been a risk taker, he is very funny, and a fun person to hang out with.

His plan is to open several businesses to make a difference to help give back to our communities, make a difference in the world, and to make someone happy.

Jhonny Solano believe in giving great customer service, to help express yourself, create expression through your clothing attire, to give you the best quality printing!

Facebook and Instagram@betterwearcustomapparel

"Woman on a Mission from God"
Minister Cynthia Newell

Native of St Louis Mo, she is 41 years young, Author and life coach of R.I.S.E. & W.I.N. Is acronym Release, Internal, Struggle, Effortlessly & Walk in Newness. She has such a good heart toward Gods people, she ministers to all God's children to support the body of Christ with the gift God has given her to talk to the people to produce eternal healing, to walk in newness of life, giving God the glory in the Kingdom. She has also published three books, first book published 2009, "Oh To Tell The Story" about African American women "This Way to Sunny" collection of love poems, "Gemini Diaries" heart of a woman that captures part of herself as a woman of God spiritual growth evolving in her gift as a Prophetess, a woman going through divorce, single parenthood, getting back in the dating season, remarried and a lot of relating topic. She uses these books as a platform to more intimate conversation open topic and discussion to young men, woman, to help them deeper their spiritual connects to be more empathetic and compassionate towards one another. She thanks God for putting this on her heart to write poetry this was a way she was able to overcome generation curses on her family battling with addition spirit in her family, this inspired her to start written poetry, because this gave her a voice to express herself even through the loss of her granny mother and cousin. Due to all she has been through she is still focus on the vision God has given her,

Titus 2:2 out of this God has birth out another assignment.

The Titus 2 Workshop the older woman and younger women. God has given her to reach out to our younger generation to do workshop to help cultivate young girls ages 10 through 16 to help build more confidence and to let them know they are beautiful, and not based on what society think, and stop bullying because when she was young, she was bullied and my daughter was also bullied, so I have such a heart an compassion to help those who has been bullied trying to keep up with today's society.

That's why, she has created *Little Sisters Big Vision the will created their vision board God has for them. She also want to work with wise woman they can rise and win.* God has given her more books which is going to be a series "The Day I Found Myself" defining moments as a woman, marriage, ministry etc. ….

She has a show online Powerless to Powerful exclusive interview on Every 2nd and 4th Saturday of each month central standard time 1 pm. Pod case lesson of life help other people from feeling powerless to powerful, through the grace of God. its full of love, laughter, support and great

Daring Daughters

Titus 2:2

Minister Cynthia said she inspires herself in spite of all she has been through from God healing her from stage 3 cancer, she never had the backing and support and love she need when life had serve her some tough times. Been homeless twice , divorcee, but in spite of it all she still have love and compassion for God people to still love and do the will of God for her life and destiny.

Her goal this year is to touch and reach 100 girls and women are whatever the will of God, He has in store for her.

"Minister Cynthia is a very funny and life of the party kind of lady"

Place your ad today!

TALMAGE CHANDLER
"MORE THAN A CONQUEROR"

Talmage Chandler 19 years of age at this moment, attends college at SWIC, (Southwestern Illinois College) He will be in an upcoming feature film "Locker Room the Movie", that will be premiering August 17, 2018. Talmage said that,

He never thought he would be an actor until his mother introduce him to this movie, he tried it and began to love acting, he did not know he had it in him, until Pastor Curry a great director, cultivated him to bring out the best in him.

He never dreamed of being an actor, but after being a part of this feature film he has experience a whole new outlook on acting and began to enjoy acting.

He said his grandmother is the one who inspires him, she has a great heart always put people before her-

I ask Talmage what inspired him the most about being in the movie, he said it's going to be awesome to be seen across the world, plus it was great working with a really cool cast! His next move will be finishing college, traveling, serving our country, going to the air force, getting a house.

Talmage, has a really good heart, loyal and a great personality, like to make people laugh. He said his grandmother is the one who inspires him, she has a great heart always put people before herself and very given.

Vendors Jubilee

Looking for professional people

Now Hiring

Editors
Journalist
Marketers
Representative
TeleMarketers

Will train, no experience necessary!

Join The Team
Call schedule your interview today!

904 661-9253

VISIT OUR WEBSITE FOR APPLICATION
WWW.VENDORSJUBILEE.COM

SCENES FROM "LOCKER ROOM THE MOVIE"

For Advertising information please contact our Advertising Department @ vendorsjubileemagazine@gmail.com
www.vendorsjubilee.com

Christian Film Director: "Locker Room The Movie

He wrote this movie while driving to Iowa to get his daughter from college on the High thinking and not knowing it was going to be a movie. It's really dealing with a young man and teens dealing with anger, rebellion, religions, bullying atheists and every aspect of life. This movie is going to reach multi culture. The devil doesn't pick color he wants souls. It doesn't matter what color you are, God created us in his image, it's not about the color of your skin it's about you are in the Kingdome of God.

Mr. Curry think he is truly a comedian who like to make people smile and put a smile on people face. Who is a very loving being and who is a chef and loves to cook. His desire is to reach and help save as many people God has in store for him to reach for the Kingdom of God.

He has accomplished many dreams God has given him but the most accomplishment of them all is to save soul. He said he believe he is the Hulk to break every spiritual bondage from God people sometimes he feels that the weight is on his shoulders, so he had to learn to turn it over to God. He said the people in his life inspires him first his wonderful wife really encourages him she is my rib, son, daughters, mother, his family without them and God he would be nothing.

You can purchase all his books on any online book store.

Locker Room The Movie Cast

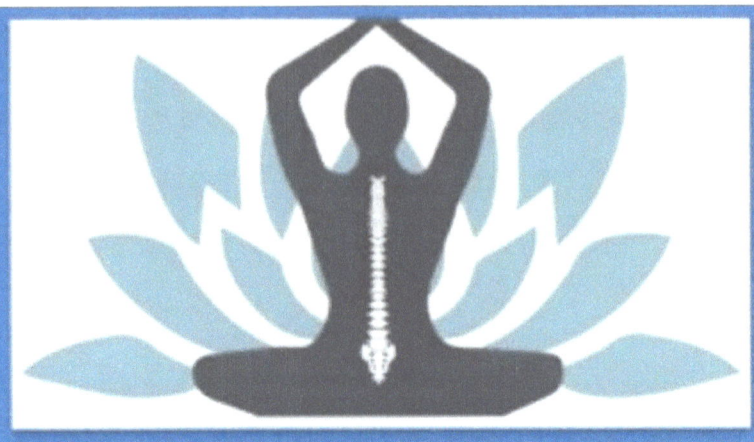

Nikki Stewart-Weiss, DC, MS
Doctor of Chiropractic
Nutrition Specialist
Independent Contractor

Phone: 636-379-1779 ext. 1022
Fax: 636-634-3496

Email:
nikki.stewart-weiss@sandhillcounseling.com

801 S. Woodlawn Avenue, Suite 15,
O'Fallon, MO 63366

www.sandhillcounseling.com

Casey Howliet
"Pursuing Your Destiny"

Casey Howliet age 19 a native from O'Fallon IL, she has always been a part of the theater in High School, never dream of being an actress and auditioning for "Locker Room The Movie" really took her out of her comfort zone, but the experience was well worth it. In spite having to learn the script had its challenges, but she pursues and was determining to perfect her role in this movie.

Her future goal is to go to college, start her on business, home realtor, and an entrepreneur.

At this moment she is working at a daycare, her passion come from her uncle and grandmother to be an entrepreneur. They have been very positive role model in her life, encouraging her to finish school to be a positive role model to her peers.

She is planning on finishing her some online college course, traveling and pursuing more acting opportunities. Go check her out "Locker Room The Movie" coming soon to a theater near you!

(On the set of "Locker Room The Movie")

"Her future goal is to go to college, start her on business, home realtor, and an entrepreneur".

"Locker Room The Movie" Coming soon to a theatre near you!

Pastor Joseph M. Curry
"Man, with A Vision"

Pastor Joseph M. Curry is a native of East St Louis IL, he is a pastor, writer, and film director and his greatest thing is to be a husband.

He knew he was going to be a pastor when God came to him in a serious of three dreams back to back, the church he went to visit, it was the same church God showed him in his dream. He prayed about it and talk to the pastor of that church and he knew this was the place it was like it felt like fire shut up in his bones like Jeremiah. He felt like Jonah in the dream. God inspired him to write books, he said God is the Author and he just the tool God use to write his books it's a message God wanted his people to hear. He said he's not superman, the Bible said in Philippians 4:13 "I can do all this through him who gives me strength." He wants to least reach one soul at a time for the Kingdom of God.

The projects he is working on now, he has so much on his plate after finishing "Locker Room The Movie". Waiting on the world premiere of this feature film. He is working on his seventh book, comic book and more feature films.

His focus is to go out and deliver God people, he feels like he is a beacon of light for God to go and help delivered God people from demonic bondage. God has given him some effective tools in his books. "Breakthrough into your Victory," Under Construction God is Rebuilding Men," Getting in Shape with God A Spiritual Workout," Clocking in for the Kingdom of God," Breaking the Chains of Demonic Bondage," and Coffee House Christian." Sounds funny but it's reality.

With all the work he has accomplish its harvest time, because these are seed that's has been planted. God has put him in his field to tend his Gardener, that s his desire. God has put him he his Spiritual garden to tend it for him.

"Pastor, Author, Visionary"

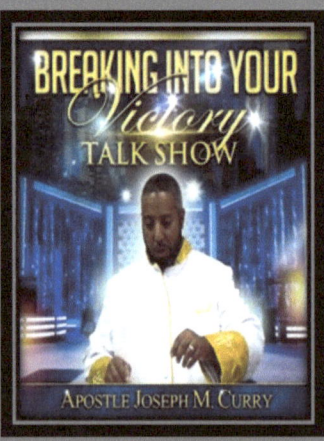

"Gabrielle Union, Taraji P. Henson are a great inspiration to her because they are independent and a very strong black role models. She also admires Snoop Dog, because he so laid back and always giving to the communities".

(Scene from "Locker Room The Movie")

Lyric Chantel

"Destine to Win"

Lyric Chantel 18 years of age a native form Belleville IL, been a cheerleader all her life. Always been into hair make up and at this moment in cosmetology school. Her dream is to build her on brand and image sell hair, be a barber, on clothing line and new fragrance, always wanted to be an actress.

Her friends told her they were casting for Locker Room The Movie, so she audition and go the part. She always wanted to be in a movie and always knew it was destining to happen. Accepting this actress role for this movie has taught me a lot of dos and don'ts when it comes to filming, like looking at the camera and really becoming the character I was acting I had to learn how to become that character at that moment and not just act it out.

I have always wanted to be an actress and model, people would always say I am a drama queen, always have something to say, very opinion-

I LOVE ♥ FASHION

ated and bold.

Her future goal is to do modeling shows, focus on her hairline, and hopefully do part 2 for Locker Room The Movie.

Her friend will say she is very loud, opinionated, out spoken, bold, funny and goofy.

She said Gabrielle Union, Taraji P. Henson are a great inspiration to her because they are independent and a very strong black role models. She also admires Snoop Dog, because he so laid back and always giving to the communities.

Her new project she is focusing on is  being a model and her hairline and she said go check her out in Locker Room The Movie coming soon August 17, 2018.

www.ingramcontent.com/pod-product-compliance
Lightning Source LLC
Chambersburg PA
CBHW051828210526
45473CB00005B/1786